I want to be a Doctor

I WANT TO BE A
Doctor

DAN LIEBMAN

FIREFLY BOOKS

A Firefly Book

Published by Firefly Books Ltd. 2000

Ninth Printing, 2013

National Library of Canada Cataloguing in Publication Data
Liebman, Daniel
    I want to be a doctor

ISBN-13: 978-1-55209-463-1 (bound)
ISBN-10: 1-55209-463-4 (bound)
ISBN-13: 978-1-55209-461-7 (pbk.)
ISBN-10: 1-55209-461-8 (pbk.)

1. Physicians – Juvenile literature.   I. Title

R690.L53 2000   j610.69'52   C99-932467-5

Published in Canada by
Firefly Books Ltd.
50 Staples Avenue, Unit 1
Richmond Hill, Ontario L4B 0A7

U.S. Cataloging-in-Publication Data
Liebman, Daniel
    I want to be a doctor/Daniel Liebman.—
1st ed. [24] p. : col. ill. ; cm. –(I want to be)
Summary : Photographs of doctors at work with short descriptive captions.
ISBN-13: 978-1-55209-463-1 (bound)
ISBN-10: 1-55209-463-4 (bound)
ISBN-13: 978-1-55209-461-7 (pbk.)
ISBN-10: 1-55209-461-8 (pbk.)
1. Physicians – Vocational guidance.
2. Occupations   I. Title   II. Series.
610.69/52/023 –dc21   2000   CIP

Published in the United States by
Firefly Books (U.S.) Inc.
P.O. Box 1338, Ellicott Station
Buffalo, New York, USA   14205

Photo Credits

© Royalty Free/Getty Images, première de couverture
© Tom & Dee Ann McCarthy/CORBIS, page 5
© Bob Krist/CORBIS, page 6
© Elizabeth Hathon/CORBIS, page 7
© Roy Morsch/CORBIS, pages 8-9
© Warren Morgan/CORBIS, pages 10, 24, quatrième de couverture
© William Taufic/CORBIS, page 11
© David H. Wells/CORBIS, page 12

© Michael Pole/CORBIS, page 13
© Vivian Moos/CORBIS, page 14
© Roger Ressmeyer/CORBIS, page 15
© Gabe Palmer/CORBIS, page 16
© Tom Stewart/CORBIS, pages 17, 19
© Brian Leng/CORBIS, page 18
© Kit Kittle/CORBIS, page 20
© Robert Garvey/CORBIS, page 21
© Ariel Skelley/CORBIS, page 22
© Chuck Savage/CORBIS, page 23

Design by Interrobang Graphic Design Inc.
Printed and bound in the United States of America

The publisher gratefully acknowledges the financial support for our publishing program by the Government of Canada through the Canada Book Fund as administered by the Department of Canadian Heritage.

Doctors help you stay healthy. When you're not well, they help you feel better.

Getting a shot is no fun. But it only hurts a little bit — and it can help you feel better fast.

A strong light helps this doctor check the baby's ear.

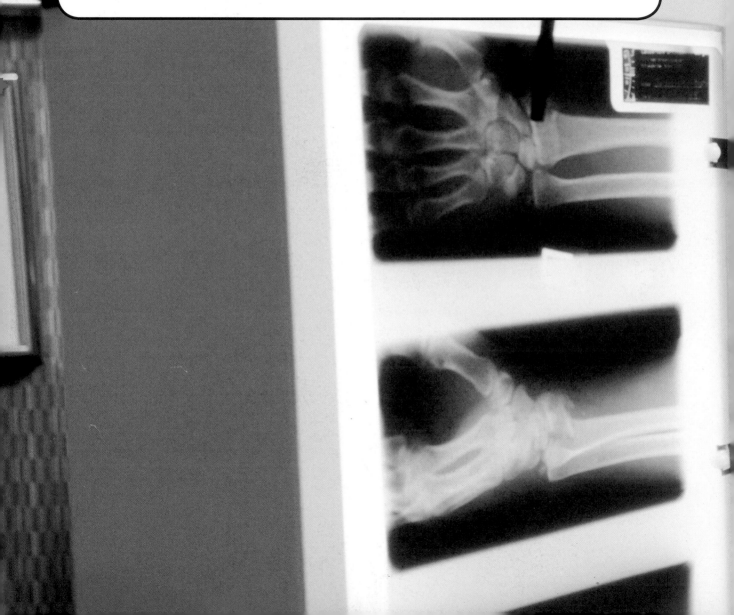

X-rays show doctors what your body looks like under the skin. The doctor is checking for broken bones.

If you break a bone, the doctor puts on a cast until the bone heals.

Hospitals can be scary. Playrooms help to make them more fun.

You slide right inside this special machine. It lets doctors see what is happening inside your body.

Doctors are gentle and kind to their patients.

Patients sometimes have to be very brave. This girl needs oxygen to help her breathe.

This doctor carefully scrubs his hands before touching the patient. It is important that germs do not spread from one person to another in the hospital.

Hospitals keep careful records for each patient. Records help doctors see how the patient is doing.

This boy is exercising his legs to make the muscles grow strong again.

Some hospitals have special rooms and equipment to help them care for children.

This man is having an operation on his wrist. A doctor who performs operations is called a surgeon.

This nurse is showing the patient an x-ray while he is being flown to the hospital in an air ambulance.

Patients are strapped in carefully to prevent injury while flying.

Paramedics take care of people in emergencies and rush them to the hospital.

Regular checkups help people stay healthy. This machine measures blood pressure.

Time to go home! Everyone is happy to know that the patient is well again.